When the World Forgot to Listen

A Journey Back to Soul, Silence, and Synchronicity

The Great Remembering
Book 1

TheReal Rayster

About the Author

TheReal Rayster is the author of *When the World Forgot to Listen*, the first book in The Great Remembering Series, and the spiritual memoir *Trance Formation*.

With a background in Computer Science and years in corporate environments, he understands firsthand the challenges of living authentically while navigating traditional career paths. After experiencing the "soul ache" that many modern professionals know well—the persistent feeling that something deeper was calling—he embarked on a transformative journey involving extensive travel, spiritual practices including Vipassana meditation, and ultimately leaving the traditional path to follow his authentic voice.

His writing bridges the gap between corporate life and spiritual awakening, offering practical wisdom for sensitive souls navigating a noisy world. His mission is to remind readers of the wisdom they already carry within, offering gentle guidance back to their authentic selves. Through personal story woven with universal truths, he creates doorways for readers to remember their own inner guidance.

When the World Forgot to Listen is the first in a four-book series exploring humanity's journey back to authentic living through listening, feeling, creating, and connecting.

Connect with him on social media @therealrayster.

Copyright © 2025 TheReal Rayster

All rights reserved. No part of this book may be reproduced, stored in a retrieval system, or transmitted in any form or by any means—electronic, mechanical, photocopying, recording, or otherwise—without the prior written permission of the copyright owner, except for brief quotations used in reviews or critical articles.

To request permissions, contact the author at:

therealrayster25@gmail.com

Some names and identifying details in this book have been changed to protect the privacy of individuals.

The information contained in this book is for general informational purposes only. It is not intended as a substitute for professional medical or psychological advice and should not be relied upon as such.

Contents

Author's Note	ix
The Silence You've Been Avoiding Is the Answer You Seek	xi
1. The Noise We Call Normal	1
2. When Spirit Became Background Noise	10
3. The Yearning You Can't Explain	17
4. The Breaking Point	23
5. The Day the Signs Returned	31
6. Listening Like the Ancients Did	38
7. Reclaiming the Forgotten Language	45
8. The Courage to Trust Again	52
9. Creating from a Listening Heart	62
10. Sacred Rebels, Soft Warriors	67
11. When the World Starts to Listen Again	72
Review Request	79
References & Sources	81

Author's Note

When I started writing this book, I had a completely different vision. Fresh from publishing *TranceFormation*, I thought I was creating a straightforward guide about finding your life's purpose—something practical and clear that would help people figure out their next steps.

But the more I wrote, the more uncomfortable I became with that approach.

Sitting with my laptop, trying to craft another framework or system, I kept thinking about how overwhelming it feels to be constantly told what we should do, how we should live, what success should look like. I realized I was about to add my voice to an already crowded conversation, and something about that just didn't feel right.

So I took a different path.

Instead of telling you what your purpose is, I found myself writing about the art of listening to what you already know. Instead of offering another set of instructions to follow, these pages became an invitation to trust the guidance that's already whispering to you.

What emerged was something I never planned—a book that asks you to tune out the noise (including mine, when necessary) and tune into the quiet wisdom that lives in your own heart. It became less about following any prescribed path and more about remembering that you already have everything you need to find your way.

I suppose that's what happens when you try to write authentically—the book ends up teaching you as much as it might teach anyone else.

If reading these words helps you trust yourself a little more deeply, listen to your own knowing a little more clearly, or feel a little more confident in the path that calls to you, then this book has done exactly what it was meant to do.

Your inner wisdom knows things no book can teach. I'm just honored to remind you to listen to it.

With gratitude and respect,
TheReal Rayster

The Silence You've Been Avoiding Is the Answer You Seek

There's a sound beneath all sounds—a whisper older than words, quieter than breath, more persistent than heartbeat. It's the voice your soul uses when it needs to tell you something important. The voice that knows things before your mind catches up. The voice that remembers who you were before the world taught you who to be.

Most of us have learned to drown it out.

We fill the spaces with notifications and news cycles, with productivity and small talk, with anything loud enough to convince us we're too busy to hear what's been trying to reach us all along. We mistake the constant hum of busyness for the music of a life well-lived.

But silence isn't emptiness. It's fullness—pregnant with possibility, rich with wisdom, alive with the sacred intelligence that flows through everything when we remember how to receive it.

This book is about that remembering. It's about returning to an ancient way of being that your ancestors

The Silence You've Been Avoiding Is the Answer You Seek

knew instinctively: the art of listening with your whole self. Not just to words, but to signs. Not just to others, but to the quiet knowing that lives in your bones. Not just to what is, but to what wants to emerge through you.

It's about discovering that the silence you've been avoiding isn't a void to be filled, but a conversation you've been invited to join.

This journey unfolds in three movements, like a song returning to its original key:

First, we must understand how we lost our way—how the noise we call normal drowned out the whispers of wisdom, how spirit became background noise in a world obsessed with speed and productivity. We'll explore the soul ache that so many of us carry, that unnamed longing for something deeper, and recognize the breaking points that force us to change.

Then, we remember what we've forgotten—learning to read the signs again, to trust the inner knowing that never actually left, to hear the ancient conversations our souls have been having all along. We'll discover how to listen beneath the surface, how to follow the threads of synchronicity, and how to let our sensitivity become our guide.

Finally, we become the bridges—living between the old world and the new, translating silence into action, sensitivity into service, carrying forward the remembering for those who come after us. We'll explore what it means to create from a listening heart and to be sacred rebels in a world that's forgotten how to hear.

What if everything you've been seeking has been

The Silence You've Been Avoiding Is the Answer You Seek

waiting for you in the quiet spaces between thoughts? What if your sensitivity isn't a weakness, but a superpower? What if the very thing that makes you feel different is the gift the world needs most?

This isn't a manual for escaping the modern world—it's an invitation to remember what's always been here, humming beneath the noise, calling you home to yourself.

The conversation begins now.

Will you listen?

Chapter 1
The Noise We Call Normal

The first notification arrives before your eyes fully open. A gentle buzz from the nightstand, then another, then the cascade begins. Email, Instagram, WhatsApp, news alerts—each one a small demand on your attention, a tiny tug on the thread of your consciousness before you've even remembered who you are in the quiet space between sleeping and waking.

By the time your feet hit the floor, you're already plugged in. Scrolling through headlines while coffee brews, checking messages while brushing teeth, consuming information and opinions and updates at a pace that would have overwhelmed our ancestors' entire lifetime. This is how we begin each day now: not with silence or reflection or the simple awareness of being alive, but with the immediate immersion into everyone else's urgency.

We tell ourselves this is normal. We call it staying informed, staying connected, staying productive. We've convinced ourselves that the constant hum of digital stimulation is the soundtrack of a life well-lived, that empty moments are problems to be solved rather than spaces to be savored.

But what if we've gotten it backwards?

What if the very thing we think is keeping us connected is actually drowning out the most important conversation of our lives—the one with ourselves?

I used to measure my worth in notifications. The more messages waiting, the more I mattered. The busier my calendar, the more successful I felt. For over a decade, I wore exhaustion like a badge of honor, the permanent background hum of anxiety like a productivity tool that kept me moving, achieving, climbing toward a definition of success I'd never questioned.

The wake-up call came disguised as loss—not just of a job, but of something harder to name. Sitting in my apartment one evening, surrounded by the accumulated symbols of a life I'd built according to someone else's blueprint, I realized I couldn't remember the last time I'd sat in actual silence. Even alone, I was never truly alone. My laptop screen glowed with endless browser tabs and streaming distractions, my phone buzzed with the hunger of applications designed to capture attention, my mind churned through tomorrow's meetings and yesterday's regrets.

The quiet, when I finally found it, was terrifying. My chest tightened as if I'd been holding my breath for years. In the space between thoughts, between distractions, something was waiting. Not emptiness, as I'd feared, but a presence I'd forgotten existed. A voice that had been trying to reach me through years of digital static and cultural noise, whispering truths my productive self was too busy to hear.

That voice knew things my resume didn't. It remembered dreams I'd filed away as impractical, felt connections I couldn't quantify on a spreadsheet, sensed possibilities that had nothing to do with quarterly targets or performance reviews. It was the part of me that had always existed but rarely got airtime in a world that rewarded doing over being, having over feeling, knowing over wondering.

The strangest part wasn't discovering this voice existed—it was realizing how hard I'd worked to drown it out.

We live in the first era in human history where silence has become uncomfortable. Our great-grandparents knew the rhythm of sunrise and sunset, the significance of seasonal changes, the way their bodies felt in different weather. They made decisions based on dreams and hunches and the way wind moved through trees. Not because they were primitive, but because they understood that human intelligence extends far beyond the rational mind.

They lived in conversation with forces we've forgotten how to perceive—the subtle energies of place and season, the wisdom that comes through symbol and synchronicity, the guidance that emerges from stillness rather than stimulation. They trusted their bodies' knowing, honored their dreams, paid attention to signs that our culture has dismissed as coincidence or wishful thinking.

Somewhere along the way, we traded this ancient partnership for something we convinced ourselves was better: the illusion of control through constant information. Now we check our phones over 90 times per day, consume vastly more information daily than previous generations, and find ourselves connected to more people and data than any humans in history—yet rates of anxiety, depression, and existential emptiness continue to climb.

The irony is profound: in our quest to stay informed about everything happening everywhere, we've become strangers to what's happening within our own bodies, our own hearts, our own souls.

Consider the last time you sat without any form of entertainment or stimulation. No book, no music, no phone, no television, no conversation—just you and the present moment. If you're like most people, you either can't remember such a moment, or the memory makes you slightly uncomfortable.

We've been conditioned to believe that unstimulated time is wasted time. Productivity culture has convinced us that value lies in constant output, that our worth is measured by our ability to generate, consume, and respond. The idea of simply being—without purpose, without agenda, without measurable result—feels foreign, almost transgressive.

But our nervous systems are paying the price. We're running on the adrenaline of perpetual emergency, treating every notification as urgent, every decision as critical, every moment as a problem to be solved rather than an experience to be lived. The constant stimulation isn't just overwhelming our minds—it's drowning out the subtle signals our bodies and intuition use to communicate wisdom.

How can we hear the whisper of inspiration over the roar of information? How can we sense the gentle guidance of instinct when we're always plugged into external input? We've created a world where the most important conversations—the ones with our deeper selves, our creative spirits, our souls' authentic desires—can barely get a word in edgewise.

Yet ancient cultures understood something we've forgotten: that wisdom often arrives in silence. The Celtic concept of thin places—locations where the veil between worlds grows gossamer-light—always involved stillness, space, the absence of human noise. Indigenous traditions included periods of solitude and quiet as essential rites of passage, times when young people would sit in silence until their true purpose revealed itself. The Desert Fathers and Mothers retreated to the Egyptian wilderness not to escape the world, but to hear it more clearly.

These weren't primitive people who simply hadn't discovered better ways to spend their time. They were sophisticated civilizations that recognized something our hyper-connected age has overlooked: that the quality of our external lives depends entirely on the depth of our internal awareness. They knew that breakthrough insights rarely arrive during busy moments, that creative solutions emerge from spaciousness rather than pressure, that the answers we seek most desperately often come through the very silence we're most afraid to enter.

Meanwhile, we've built a civilization that profits from our distraction. Social media platforms employ teams of neuroscientists to make their products addictive. News cycles trigger fight-or-flight responses that keep us scrolling. Advertising algorithms study our behavior to predict and influence our desires before we're even conscious of them.

We're not just victims of this system—we're willing participants in our own disconnection. We reach for our phones during every moment of potential boredom, fill every drive with background noise to avoid silence, schedule ourselves so tightly that reflection becomes impossible. We've made busyness a virtue and stillness a luxury we can't afford.

Perhaps most insidiously, our noise-addicted culture has convinced us that our inner voice—if it exists at all—can't be trusted. We've been taught to seek validation from external sources: experts, influencers, data points, social media likes. The idea that we might contain our own guidance system, that our bodies and intuition might know things our minds haven't learned, seems quaint at best, delusional at worst.

The result is a strange form of modern loneliness: surrounded by information but starved for wisdom, connected to everyone but ourselves, busy beyond measure but somehow missing the very life we're trying so hard to manage.

What would change if we remembered that silence isn't emptiness but fullness? That the space between thoughts isn't a void to be filled but fertile ground where new possibilities take root? That the uncomfortable feeling we get when all the distractions fall away isn't boredom but the return of our authentic selves, asking to be heard?

Our ancestors knew that certain kinds of knowledge only come through certain kinds of attention. The farmer who could predict weather by the behavior of birds wasn't guessing—she was reading information invisible to those who hadn't learned to look. The indigenous tracker who could follow a trail days old wasn't using supernatural powers—he was accessing sensory awareness we've forgotten we possess.

These abilities haven't disappeared; they've simply been buried under layers of digital stimulation and cultural conditioning that convinces us to trust everything except our own direct experience.

What if your anxiety isn't a disorder but a messenger, trying to tell you something important about how you're living? What if your chronic dissatisfaction isn't ingratitude but your soul's way of saying you're capable of more than you're currently expressing? What if the dreams you've dismissed as unrealistic are actually intelligence from a part of you that sees further than your fear?

What if the very sensitivity you've learned to hide—your ability to feel deeply, to sense the emotional undercurrents in rooms, to be moved by beauty in ways others might find excessive—isn't a weakness but a gift? What if you're not too much, but living in a world that's become too little, too numb, too disconnected from the very qualities that make us most human? What if your restlessness isn't disorder but your soul's way of calling you back to what you've forgotten?

The path back to listening begins with a radical recognition: that the voice you've been taught to question is the only one that truly knows the way home. Not home to a physical place, but home to yourself. Home to the person you were before the world taught you who to be. Home to the dreams you had before you learned they were impractical. Home to the wisdom you possessed before you were convinced you needed to seek it elsewhere.

This isn't about abandoning reason or retreating from the world. It's about remembering that there are many ways of knowing, and the one we've prioritized—logical, linear, measurable—is only one instrument in the orchestra of human intelligence. It's about discovering that the rational mind, for all its gifts, was never meant to be a dictator but a collaborator, working in harmony with intuition, creativity, and the mysterious intelligence that flows through our bodies and our dreams.

It's about reclaiming silence not as an absence but as a presence. Not as empty space waiting to be filled but as pregnant possibility, rich with the very guidance we've been seeking in all the wrong places.

The conversation begins with a simple, revolutionary

act: turning down the volume on everything else so you can finally hear the voice that's been calling your name all along.

In a world that profits from your distraction, choosing to listen to yourself is the ultimate rebellion. In a culture that has forgotten how to be still, your silence becomes a sacred act. In an age that has lost touch with mystery, your willingness to trust what you cannot prove but somehow know becomes a bridge back to ancient wisdom.

The world needs people who remember how to listen. It needs your particular way of sensing and feeling and knowing. It needs your willingness to honor what moves you, even when you can't explain why. It needs your courage to follow the thread of your curiosity, even when it leads somewhere your practical mind never planned to go.

Most of all, it needs you to remember that beneath all the noise—digital and cultural and mental—something vast and intelligent and unutterably loving has been waiting patiently for you to come home to yourself.

But first, you must understand exactly how we lost our way. How the very signs that once guided us became background noise. How spirit itself learned to whisper in a world that had forgotten how to listen.

The conversation begins now. Will you follow it deeper?

Chapter 2
When Spirit Became Background Noise

The coffee shop breathes with the familiar rhythm of modern life—espresso machines exhaling steam like sighs, keyboards tapping out urgent messages to nowhere in particular, phones buzzing with the relentless hunger of applications that feed on attention. The air carries the scent of burnt coffee and ambition, mingled with the faint sweetness of pastries cooling behind glass.

A woman at the corner table moves her thumb in practiced meditation across her phone screen, searching. Always searching. She's been asking the universe for a sign about her direction, praying for guidance about the emptiness that's been following her like a shadow. Just this morning she lit a candle and whispered, "Show me what I'm supposed to do next." Now she scrolls through spiritual quotes and self-help posts, hunting for the answer that feels increasingly elusive, while beside her, steam rises from her untouched latte like incense from a forgotten altar.

Three feet away, an elderly man sits in the kind of stillness that remembers other centuries, watching a robin tap at the window with peculiar persistence. Tap, tap, tap—three times, four times, five. Each knock deliberate as prayer, purposeful as prophecy. His weathered hands rest calmly on his walking stick, and there's something in his posture that speaks of generations who knew how to read the world differently. He doesn't pull out a phone to Google "what does it mean when a bird taps on window." He doesn't dismiss it as random animal behavior. Instead, he watches with the patient attention of someone who learned from his grandmother that robins carry messages about change, about new beginnings trying to break through old patterns.

The woman never looks up. Her phone buzzes—a text from a forgotten friend carrying an invitation to the very workshop that will ignite her spiritual awakening—and she glances at it with the same distracted swipe she gives everything else. She's so busy hunting for signs online that she misses the robin's message, so focused on finding guidance in other people's words that she overlooks the answer arriving in real time. The universe has responded to her morning prayer, but her attention is everywhere except the present moment where spirit actually lives.

The old man smiles quietly, recognizing the ancient dance: spirit offering exactly what's needed while modern souls look everywhere except where the gift is being given. He's witnessed this same scene play out countless times—the hungry seeking what's already present, the lost ignoring the directions being offered, the spiritually starved scrolling past the feast spread before them.

This is how we miss it. This is how spirit slips past us, disguised as ordinary moments, while we're busy seeking it everywhere except where it actually appears. Two people, both hungry for connection to something greater than themselves, but only one present enough to receive what's being offered.

We do this everywhere, in ways both subtle and obvious. The businessman who prays every morning for guidance about his struggling marriage, then spends his commute on calls, missing the radio song that his wife used to sing, the billboard advertising the marriage workshop she mentioned last month, the coffee shop where they had their first date—now advertising couples' nights.

The college student desperately seeking her life purpose, scrolling through career advice while the elderly woman next to her on the bus carries a tote bag from the exact nonprofit she's been dreaming of joining. The woman even strikes up a conversation about the organization's mission, but the student has earbuds in, lost in someone else's wisdom about finding her calling.

The mother feeling overwhelmed and alone, asking for strength while standing in the grocery store checkout line, as the magazine cover in front of her features an article about the exact parenting strategy she needs—but she's busy texting about her stress instead of noticing what's literally in front of her face.

We've learned to seek guidance everywhere except in the present moment where it's actually being offered. We hunt for signs while ignoring them, pray for direction while looking away from the responses, ask for help while tuning out the universe's attempts to provide it.

But perhaps even more heartbreaking are the moments when we do sense something—when the guidance arrives not through external signs but as an inner knowing, a gentle pull, a sudden certainty about what we need to do—and we dismiss it. We talk ourselves out of it. We let fear or logic or social conditioning override the very wisdom we've been praying to receive.

You know this feeling. The sudden urge to call an old friend, dismissed as random nostalgia, only to discover later that they were going through a crisis and desperately needed to hear from someone who cared. The impulse to take a different route to work, overruled by efficiency, missing the coffee shop where you would have met the person with the answer to your biggest professional challenge.

The unexpected excitement about a creative project that seemed impractical, so you filed it away under "someday" and watched someone else birth a similar vision to great success. The pull to speak to the interesting stranger at the bookstore, dismissed as inappropriate, never knowing that brief conversation could have led to love, friendship, or the collaboration that would have changed everything.

The feeling in your chest that said "apply for this," even though you didn't meet all the qualifications, overruled by the voice that insisted you weren't ready, weren't worthy, weren't enough. The quiet knowing that whispered "this relationship isn't right for you," buried under the noise of what looked good on paper, what made sense to everyone else, what you thought you should want.

These moments accumulate like sediment in the soul, layer upon layer of discounted intuition, dismissed guidance, ignored inner knowing. Each time we choose logic over intuition, safety over soul-prompting, we create a little more distance between ourselves and the part of us that actually knows the way forward. Each dismissed whisper makes the next one harder to hear, until eventually we find ourselves spiritually homesick—aching for something we can't name, seeking something we've forgotten how to recognize.

The tragedy isn't that we make wrong choices—it's that we've learned to doubt the very guidance system we were born with, the internal compass that knows things our minds haven't learned yet, that senses possibilities our rational selves can't see. We've been taught that wisdom comes from outside ourselves, that our hunches aren't trustworthy, that being spiritual means looking to others for what we should trust, believe, or feel.

This isn't our fault. Somewhere along the way, we forgot that the world is always speaking to us through the most ordinary channels. We lost the understanding that spirit doesn't usually arrive through burning bushes or booming voices, but through the gentle persistence of robins tapping on windows, through conversations overheard at just the right moment, through doors that open exactly when we need them to.

But more than that, we've been systematically trained out of trusting our own inner guidance. From childhood, we learn to defer to external authorities—parents, teachers, experts, social media influencers—rather than developing confidence in our own ability to sense what's true, what's right, what's calling us forward. We're taught that following hunches is risky, that trusting gut feelings is naive, that real adults make decisions based on data and logic, not on the mysterious stirrings of the heart.

The result is a peculiar form of modern suffering: surrounded by more information than any humans in history, yet starved for wisdom. Connected to countless voices through our devices, yet disconnected from the one voice that actually knows what we need. We have access to every spiritual teaching ever recorded, yet we've forgotten how to listen to the teacher that lives within our own bones.

The irony is profound: in our quest to find meaning, we miss the meaning that's already present. In our search for guidance, we overlook the guidance that's already being offered. In our hunger for connection to something greater than ourselves, we fail to notice that we're already held, already supported, already part of a conversation that never stops.

The universe hasn't stopped speaking. We've just forgotten that we're part of the conversation. But forgetting isn't permanent. And sometimes the ache of what we're missing becomes so acute that we finally become willing to stop seeking long enough to start receiving.

Sometimes the very emptiness we've been trying to fill becomes the doorway to remembering what we've always known but learned to doubt. Sometimes the yearning itself becomes the compass that points us back to the conversation we never actually left.

The next tap on the window might be the one that finally gets our attention. The next inner prompting might be the one we finally trust. The next moment of guidance might be the one that reminds us we were never as lost as we thought—we were just looking in all the wrong places for something that was always, always here.

Chapter 3
The Yearning You Can't Explain

Three in the morning, and sleep has abandoned her again. She lies in the darkness of her suburban bedroom, moonlight casting long shadows across furniture that once felt like home but now feels like a beautiful prison. Her husband's breathing maintains its steady rhythm beside her—the good man she chose because he was stable, reliable, everything her parents said she should want.

But something in her chest feels like it's slowly suffocating.

She thinks about the art studio she never rented, the creative writing program she talked herself out of applying to, the photography project that still lives in a folder on her laptop marked "Someday." She remembers the woman who once dreamed of living in a small coastal town, running a gallery, traveling to document stories that mattered. But practical voices won—her mother's concerns about financial security, society's timeline for marriage and children, the sensible choice to build a life that looked successful on paper.

Down the hall, her children sleep peacefully in beds she carefully chose. She loves them fiercely, but even that love can't fill the growing emptiness where her authentic self used to live. The mortgage payment clears automatically each month for the house that symbolizes everything she worked toward. The promotion she fought for has settled into routine responsibilities that feel increasingly meaningless.

She should be grateful. She has everything she's supposed to want. So why does she feel like she's disappearing?

Around the world, others share her midnight questioning. Last week, a friend called me on my birthday. Between congratulations and catching up, she mentioned almost casually feeling depressed despite booking her dream trip to Europe. "I should be excited," she said, her voice thin as tissue paper, "but I just feel empty."

Another friend has been gaining weight steadily, not from illness but from what he describes as "just not caring anymore." He moves through days on autopilot, making decisions that feel predetermined. "I feel like I don't have any real choices," he told me recently. "Like I'm going through the motions until something changes, but I don't know what."

These aren't isolated cases of depression. These are symptoms of soul starvation—the gradual withering that occurs when we live too far from our authentic selves for too long.

When the World Forgot to Listen

I know this yearning because it lived in my chest for years. After the promotion I'd worked toward, I found myself sitting with an associate manager in a conference room on the 11th floor. We were waiting on a call, and I stared through the glass overlooking the city below.

In that moment, surrounded by everything that should have felt like success, one thought kept circling through my mind: "Is this something I really want to do with my life?" I had this growing feeling that this wasn't for me—this role, this trajectory, this version of success. But I didn't know what to do about it, or what else I even wanted instead.

I wasn't successful—I was successful at being someone I wasn't.

The yearning isn't pathology—it's prophecy. Your soul remembering who you were before the world taught you who to be.

This recognition often arrives when external circumstances suggest it shouldn't. When you finally get the promotion, the relationship, the house you've been seeking, and discover that achieving what you thought you wanted only makes the hollowness more obvious. The very success that was supposed to fill the ache instead illuminates how deep it actually goes.

The yearning speaks through inexplicable attraction to beauty that breaks your heart open—a sunset that stops you in your tracks, music that moves you to tears for reasons you can't articulate, art that makes you feel homesick for a place you've never been. These aren't random emotional responses—they're recognitions. Your soul finding momentary expression through experiences that bypass rational mind and speak directly to who you are beneath all the accumulated layers.

Our culture has trained us to dismiss these moments as impractical sentimentality. We've learned to prioritize what makes sense over what makes us come alive, to choose safety over soul-growth even when safety becomes its own prison. We've created lives so busy, so structured, so focused on external validation that there's no space for the quiet voice that knows what would actually nourish us.

But what if the very sensitivity that feels like burden is actually your greatest strength? What if the inability to settle for "good enough" isn't personal failing but soul wisdom refusing to accept less than truth? What if your restlessness isn't ingratitude but an internal compass pointing toward possibilities your practical mind hasn't discovered yet?

The yearning knows things your rational mind hasn't learned yet. It knows the difference between what looks good and what feels true, between success that impresses others and success that feeds your soul. It can sense when you're living someone else's story and remembers what your own story felt like before you learned to doubt it.

It speaks through your body's wisdom—the way certain environments make you feel instantly at home while others, no matter how impressive, leave you feeling drained. The way some conversations energize you while others, despite being perfectly pleasant, feel like wearing a mask that's slightly too tight. The way certain activities make you lose track of time in the most delicious way while others, despite being productive and important, feel like swimming upstream.

Most of all, it remembers what you've forgotten: that you are not a machine designed for maximum productivity, but a soul having a human experience. That your sensitivity isn't weakness but a gift that allows you to perceive subtleties others miss. That your restlessness isn't ingratitude but your inner compass pointing toward possibilities your practical mind can't yet imagine.

The cost of ignoring this yearning compounds over time. Each day spent living at a distance from yourself adds another layer of accumulated inauthenticity. Each choice to prioritize safety over soul-calling creates more internal pressure. Each time you silence the voice that knows what would actually nourish you, that voice grows both quieter and more desperate.

Eventually, something has to give. The gap between who you are and who you're pretending to be becomes too wide to bridge. The energy required to maintain a life that doesn't match your inner truth becomes exhausting. The yearning that started as gentle restlessness transforms into urgent necessity.

The woman lying awake at three in the morning isn't suffering from insomnia—she's receiving the call to remember herself. The friend traveling to Europe while feeling depressed isn't ungrateful—she's discovering that external experiences can't fill an internal void. The friend living on autopilot isn't lazy—he's protecting himself the only way he knows how while his soul stages a quiet rebellion.

The yearning you can't explain is your authentic self calling your name, reminding you that it's never too late to remember who you actually are. The question is: how much longer will you keep them waiting?

Chapter 4
The Breaking Point

January 11, 2023—a date forever etched in my heart.

The veterinarian's smile was all reassurance as she held up the small, chewable tablet. "This new 3-in-1 tick and flea preventative will be perfect for her," she said, gesturing toward Raychel, our tiny Japanese Spitz whose fluffy white coat had earned countless admirers during our rare outings. I hesitated—Raychel had always been stubborn about medications—but the vet's confidence was persuasive.

That night seemed normal. Raychel even gobbled down all her food, happy to be part of our family dinner. Then, hours later, my mother's piercing shriek ripped through the silence: "Raychel! Raychel!!"

I found our eleven-year-old companion crumpled on the floor, her small body unnaturally still. My stepfather attempted CPR while I frantically called the vet. No answer. When Raychel finally stirred, her movements were uncoordinated, her eyes glazed, her head listing to one side. We carried her to my room, but deep down, I knew this wasn't just a simple reaction. This was the beginning of the end.

Then came the second blow: "Your Aunt B... she's gone," my mother whispered through her own grief. Two devastating losses on the same day—January 11th. The coincidence felt cosmic, cruel.

For nineteen days, I became Raychel's full-time caregiver. Work was put on hold as I monitored her every breath, administered medications, and fought against the kidney damage the vet said wouldn't heal. "Kidneys don't regenerate like the liver," she'd warned. Each day was a battle between hope and reality, between my desperate need to save her and the inevitable truth that some things are beyond our control.

The breaking point arrived at 7:45 PM on January 29th—exactly nineteen days after her first seizure, exactly the same time it had occurred. As Raychel's small body finally surrendered, I felt something shatter inside my chest that went far beyond grief. It was the recognition that the life I'd carefully constructed was as fragile as morning mist.

But the universe wasn't finished with its dismantling. A few months later, the final domino fell. My boss wanted to talk on a Monday evening—I felt a flutter of excitement, maybe another promotion? I'd received a salary increase just two months prior, and after nearly ten years with the company, my performance reviews had been stellar. Perhaps this was the recognition I'd been working toward.

The video call started casually enough. Small talk, pleasantries, the usual rhythm of professional conversation. Then, without preamble, he cut to the point: I was being laid off. The words hung in the digital space between us, surreal and incomprehensible. He seemed eager to end the conversation, rushing through logistics with the practiced efficiency of someone who'd delivered this news before, as if this kind of corporate circus was just another Tuesday.

"What... what just happened?" I whispered to my empty apartment after the call ended. Ten years. A recent raise. Stellar reviews. And now this. As I sat there, staring at the brown butterfly that had mysteriously appeared on my ceiling, I realized that the universe had systematically dismantled everything I thought gave my life meaning—and everything I thought was secure.

The breaking point isn't always a single moment—sometimes it's a series of losses that strip away every external structure until only truth remains.

My story isn't unique. Around the world, others navigate similar moments when the gap between who they've become and who they're meant to be becomes too wide to bridge. When the cost of not listening to themselves finally exceeds the cost of change.

Three time zones away, a businessman sits beside his teenage daughter who attempted suicide two weeks ago. She's recovering physically, but the emotional landscape remains treacherous. What breaks him isn't just the attempt itself but the recognition that he'd been so focused on providing for her future that he'd somehow missed her present—the signs, the silences, the way she'd been trying to tell him something important through behavior he kept interpreting as rebellion rather than desperation.

He built his entire identity around being a good father, working seventy-hour weeks to afford the private school, the violin lessons, the college fund that would give her opportunities he never had. But sitting here now, watching her sleep with bandages around her wrists, he finally understands the terrible irony: in his effort to give her everything, he'd forgotten to give her the one thing she needed most—his actual presence, his real attention, his willingness to see her as she was rather than who he hoped she would become.

Two time zones away, a woman sits in her corner office overlooking a city that once represented everything she thought she wanted. The promotion came through this morning—the one she'd been chasing for three years, the one that validates every sacrifice, every weekend worked, every relationship postponed in service of ambition. She should feel triumphant. Instead, she feels hollow, as if success itself has revealed its fundamental emptiness.

The salary increase will fund the lifestyle that requires the job that demands the sacrifices that make the lifestyle necessary—a perfect circle of sophisticated misery that masquerades as adult responsibility. As she stares at the contract that will bind her to five more years of this trajectory, this life that looks perfect from the outside but feels like a beautiful prison from within, she realizes that getting what she thought she wanted has forced her to confront what she actually needs.

This is how breaking points arrive for so many of us: not as sudden catastrophe but as the slow-motion collision between who we've become and who we've always been. Not as external crisis but as the moment when the distance between our authentic selves and our performed lives becomes too vast to bridge with explanations or good intentions.

The breaking point is where the soul finally says "enough."

But here's what makes these moments sacred rather than simply tragic: they're not endings but revelations. Not failures but fierce acts of self-love, the psyche's way of refusing to continue living at a distance from itself. They're invitations disguised as crises, opportunities wearing the mask of loss, doorways that only open when everything else falls apart.

Three days after laying Raychel to rest, I found myself writing something I'd never attempted before—a poem. The words poured out like water through a broken dam, raw and unfiltered, capturing grief in ways I didn't know language could hold. I'd never considered myself a writer, never imagined words as anything more than functional tools. But there, in the aftermath of devastating loss, something creative and essential had emerged from the wreckage. That unexpected poem would prove to be a foreshadowing of the very words you're reading now, the first whisper of an authentic voice I never knew I possessed.

The businessman will eventually learn to measure fatherhood not by what he provides but by who he shows up as. The executive will discover that real success feels different than she imagined—quieter, more grounded, aligned with values she'd forgotten she possessed.

But first, they must all pass through the fire of undoing, the necessary destruction that clears ground for what wants to grow.

This is the paradox of breaking points: they break us open precisely because we've become too closed. They shatter our carefully constructed identities because those identities have become too small to contain who we're actually meant to be. They force us to our knees because we've forgotten that surrender is sometimes the only path to freedom.

Our culture teaches us to fear these moments, to avoid them through distraction and medication and the relentless pursuit of comfort. We've been conditioned to see breakdown as failure rather than breakthrough, to interpret the end of what no longer serves as tragedy rather than liberation.

But what if the breaking point isn't the problem—what if it's the solution finally arriving?

What if your anxiety isn't pathology but prophecy, your depression not chemical imbalance but spiritual malnourishment, your restlessness not weakness but wisdom trying to redirect you toward something more aligned with your true nature?

When the World Forgot to Listen

What if the very thing you've been trying to fix is actually the thing that's trying to fix your life?

As my stepdad gently laid Raychel to rest beneath the guava tree and I later processed the shock of my sudden termination, I was forced to confront a truth I'd been avoiding: the life I'd built to impress others had become the very thing that was suffocating what mattered most. The breaking point revealed what I'd been denying—that the persistent ache in my soul wasn't weakness but wisdom, that meaning doesn't come from external achievements but from the courage to listen to the voice that knows the difference between what looks good and what feels true.

The mystics throughout history have recognized these dark nights of the soul as necessary passages on the journey toward wholeness. They understood what we've forgotten: that meaningful change requires a willingness to let something die so something else can be born. That the caterpillar doesn't gradually become a butterfly but dissolves completely in the cocoon before emerging as something entirely new.

What if this very moment is your breaking point? What if the restlessness you've been trying to manage, the dissatisfaction you've been trying to explain away, the yearning you can't quite name—what if these aren't problems to be solved but calls to be answered?

The question isn't whether you can handle what's breaking apart. The question is: are you ready to discover who you become when everything that isn't essentially you falls away?

Are you willing to find out what remains when all the roles and identities and carefully constructed personas crumble into dust?

The breaking point is where this meeting finally becomes possible. It's where the authentic self, patient as ancient trees, finally gets to speak without interference from all the voices that were never really yours—and, more importantly, where we finally remember how to listen.

And what it has to say might just change everything.

Like seeds that require the darkness of winter soil before they can push toward spring light, some kinds of knowing can only emerge from the fertile darkness of everything falling apart. The breaking point plants us deep in the earth of our own essential nature, where we finally become still enough to hear what has been growing toward us all along.

And sometimes, in that profound stillness after everything familiar has crumbled away, the first whispers of guidance begin to return—not as grand revelations, but as the gentlest of signs that something new is ready to be born.

Chapter 5
The Day the Signs Returned

The divorce papers arrive on a Tuesday morning, delivered by a courier who apologizes for the early hour as if he knows he's carrying the official end of someone's carefully constructed life. She signs for the envelope with hands that feel like they belong to someone else, thanks him with a voice that sounds remarkably steady, and closes the door on twenty-three years of marriage that somehow evaporated into legal documents and asset divisions.

But it's not the papers that break her open. It's what happens next.

Standing in her kitchen, still holding the envelope, she watches a butterfly struggle against the window glass—orange and black wings beating frantically against the transparent barrier that separates it from the garden beyond. For ten minutes, maybe fifteen, she stands transfixed by this tiny creature's desperate dance for freedom, seeing in its futile efforts a mirror of her own decades-long struggle against the invisible walls of a life that stopped fitting years ago.

Then, without warning, the butterfly stops struggling. It rests for a moment against the glass, wings spread wide like a prayer, before finding the open section of window she hadn't noticed was there. In three graceful movements, it floats into the morning air and disappears into the garden her ex-husband always said she spent too much time tending.

She breaks down then, not from grief but from recognition. The butterfly didn't force its way through the glass—it found the opening that was already there. It didn't fight the barrier until it shattered—it stopped struggling long enough to discover another way.

This is how signs return to us: not as magical intervention but as sudden clarity, the moment when what we've been unable to see becomes impossible to ignore. They arrive when our old ways of navigating the world have finally exhausted themselves, when the careful strategies that once felt so solid begin to crumble like autumn leaves, leaving us open to guidance that whispers from deeper wells.

Three time zones away, a man sits in his rental car outside the cemetery where his father lies buried beneath six months of unvisited grief. He drove here on impulse, called in sick to work for the first time in five years, following some inner compass that insisted today was the day to finally say goodbye properly. But now, staring at the wrought-iron gates, he can't make himself get out of the car.

When the World Forgot to Listen

That's when the song begins on the radio—"Blue Eyes Crying in the Rain," the Willie Nelson ballad his father hummed while shaving every Sunday morning, the tune that became the soundtrack of countless shared silences in the workshop where they rebuilt engines and occasionally, accidentally, their relationship. The DJ mentions it's a request from someone named David for his son Michael, and the man's hands tremble on the steering wheel because his name is Michael and his father's name was David and this song hasn't played on the radio in the three years since his father's death.

He could explain it away. Common names, popular song, coincidence wearing the mask of meaning. But something in his chest loosens like a fist unclenching, and he finds himself walking through those gates with the strange sensation that he's not walking alone.

The rational mind weaves elaborate explanations for such moments—confirmation bias, selective attention, the brain's hunger for patterns in a random universe. But the heart recognizes something the mind cannot quantify: the particular quality of grace that accompanies certain coincidences, the way some synchronicities feel like gifts rather than accidents, expansive rather than grasping, aligned with love rather than born from our deepest fears.

In a small college town, a teenager sits surrounded by university brochures she's supposed to be reading, but her attention keeps drifting to the same book that seems to be following her like a gentle, persistent friend. First, her favorite teacher mentioned it during an offhand comment about following unconventional paths. Then she found a copy abandoned on the bus seat beside her, left behind by someone who'd marked passages about trusting internal guidance over external expectations. Yesterday, three different people brought it up in conversations that had nothing to do with literature or career advice.

The book isn't about her intended major or even remotely related to the pre-med program her parents have planned for her future. It's about young women who changed course, who trusted their hearts over their heads, who found courage to honor gifts that didn't fit into standard categories. When she opens it randomly and finds herself reading about an artist who abandoned her law degree to paint murals in small mountain towns, she feels something electric shoot through her chest.

For months, she's been carrying a secret—applications she's filled out but never sent to art schools her parents know nothing about. Dreams she's sketched in margins when she should have been studying organic chemistry. Visions of galleries and studios that make her heart race in ways the prospect of medical school never has. She's been waiting for a sign, some external validation that it's okay to disappoint everyone who has invested in her practical future.

The book's persistence feels like conversation, like the universe finally responding to prayers she's been afraid to voice aloud. Not commanding her to make any particular choice, but reminding her that some decisions can only be made with the heart, that some paths reveal themselves only to those brave enough to follow their deepest knowing rather than their deepest fears.

When the World Forgot to Listen

Signs return when we stop demanding that guidance arrive wearing the clothes we expect, when we become humble enough to consider that intelligence might flow through channels as ordinary as radio dedications and as mysterious as the timing of abandoned books. They emerge when we're finally tired of our own noise, empty enough of manufactured certainty to hear the conversation that has been unfolding around us like morning light, patient and persistent and impossible to ignore once we remember how to see.

Our ancestors knew this. They understood that certain kinds of knowledge only arrive through certain kinds of attention, that wisdom often speaks in whispers rather than shouts, that the most important messages frequently come disguised as ordinary moments we could easily dismiss if we're not paying attention. They lived in partnership with forces our culture has forgotten how to perceive, trusting that the world itself might be a source of intelligence worth listening to.

But we've trained ourselves out of such receptivity. We've created lives so loud, so busy, so focused on manufacturing our own experiences that there's no space for the subtle guidance that once helped our grandparents navigate uncertainty with something approaching grace. We seek answers everywhere except in the present moment where they're actually being offered.

The woman with the butterfly will later describe that morning as the day she finally stopped fighting her own transformation. The man in the cemetery will play his father's song at the memorial service he organizes six months later, telling mourners about the impossible radio dedication that helped him remember love transcends death. The teenager will submit her art school applications on the anniversary of finding that book for the fourth time, trusting that some forms of knowing require no external validation.

Each will remember this as the day they stopped explaining away the very experiences that were trying to guide them home to themselves. The day they chose to receive rather than dismiss, to trust rather than doubt, to follow the thread of meaning even when they couldn't see where it led.

Signs return because consciousness extends far beyond the boundaries of individual minds, because we live in a universe that is responsive rather than random, because the intelligence that creates galaxies and guides migrating birds also weaves patterns of meaning through our daily lives for those who know how to recognize them.

They arrive not as proof of anything mystical or supernatural, but as reminders of what we've forgotten: that we belong to something larger than our individual concerns, that our deepest desires and the world's deepest needs often align in ways we couldn't orchestrate through planning alone, that guidance is always available to those who remember how to ask for it and how to recognize the answers when they come.

The day signs return is the day we finally become available to receive them. Often, it's the soul ache—that unnamed yearning we've been carrying—that finally empties us enough to listen. The restlessness that felt like suffering becomes the very thing that makes us receptive to guidance. It's the day we trade our addiction to control for trust in something more intelligent than our individual will, recognizing that the emptiness we've been trying to fill was actually creating space for what we most needed to hear.

What if this very moment is that day for you? What if your growing awareness of meaningful coincidences isn't imagination but remembering? What if the gentle persistence of certain thoughts, the impossible timing of chance encounters, the sense that something larger is trying to catch your attention—what if none of this is wishful thinking but recognition of the conversation you were always meant to join?

The signs haven't returned because they ever left. They've simply found you ready to receive them again, willing to trust what you can't prove but somehow know, brave enough to follow the golden thread of guidance that leads not to where your mind thinks you should go, but to where your soul has always known you belong.

Chapter 6
Listening Like the Ancients Did

There's a moment we all know: when your phone dies at the worst possible time, or you're somewhere with no signal, and suddenly you feel completely cut off from the world. That mild panic that rises when you realize how dependent you've become on this little device for direction, connection, and even a sense of safety. It's a modern anxiety that our ancestors would find bewildering—the fear of being alone with ourselves, of having to navigate life without constant external guidance.

I found myself face to face with this exact feeling at a forest retreat, but multiplied by a thousand. As part of the Vipassana meditation program, we had to surrender all electronic devices on the first day. No phones, no watches, no connection to the digital world that had become my constant companion. What I thought would be liberating turned into the trigger for a level of anxiety I hadn't expected.

When the World Forgot to Listen

Standing there, handing over my phone, I felt like I was losing my lifeline. That small rectangle had become more than a communication device—it was my map, my clock, my source of distraction when difficult emotions arose, my way of feeling connected to something larger than myself. Without it, I was just me, in a forest, with nowhere to hide from whatever was about to surface.

The anxiety hit immediately. My chest tightened, my breathing became shallow, and that familiar spiral of worried thoughts began: *What if something happens? What if I need help? What if I can't handle this?* I was discovering how thoroughly modern life had trained me to seek guidance outside myself, and how terrifying it felt to be thrown back on my own inner resources.

Seeing my distress, Marcus, one of the retreat staff, offered to get help for me. "This isn't unusual, especially for first-timers," he said with concern. "Let me talk to the Teacher." When he returned, he simply said, "The Teacher will see you now."

Sitting on the porch of the White Hall with the teacher, I poured out my anxiety and fear. Instead of offering complicated psychological techniques or encouraging me to push through it, he did something beautifully simple. "Let me teach you something," he said gently. "It's called Anapana—just focusing on the breath at your nostrils. Feel the coolness of air coming in, the warmth flowing out. That's all."

We practiced together for a few minutes, and I was surprised by how quickly the frantic mental noise began to settle. "The anxiety might not disappear completely," he explained, "but you now have a tool that's been helping people for over two thousand years. And the most important thing? You don't need any device for this. You carry it with you everywhere you go."

His words were both practical and profound: *You already have everything you need.* This simple breath awareness wasn't just a technique—it was a way of returning to the most fundamental guidance system humans have always possessed. Our ancestors didn't have Google Maps or weather apps, but they had something we've largely forgotten: the ability to read the subtle intelligence that flows through the body, the environment, and the present moment.

A few days later, during the deeper body scanning meditations, I began to understand why this ancient practice had persisted for millennia. As I systematically moved my attention through my body, years of stored tension and emotion began to surface and release in ways that talk therapy had never quite accessed. It was as if these old practices knew exactly how to reach the places where healing needed to happen.

Then came the real test. I woke up at midnight with the kind of terror that has no rational explanation—heart racing, breath shallow, feeling like I was drowning in my own panic. Every modern technique I'd learned for managing anxiety felt completely useless. I stumbled out of my room, desperate for help, feeling like I was falling apart completely.

Noah, one of the retreat staff, appeared in the hallway. He could have offered complex advice or tried to analyze what was happening. Instead, he simply placed his hand gently on my shoulder and said, "Remember your breath."

In that moment of complete breakdown, the ancient tool the teacher had given me became my lifeline. As I focused on the coolness entering my nostrils and the warmth flowing out, something extraordinary happened. The panic didn't disappear instantly, but I found solid ground beneath the storm. This practice that had guided humans through crisis for twenty-five hundred years was working exactly as it always had.

"This is not uncommon," Noah explained calmly. "You're releasing things that have been stuck for a long time. You showed courage by seeking help instead of trying to handle it alone." His words helped me understand that breakdown can be breakthrough, that sometimes we have to fall apart in order to remember what really holds us together.

What happened next reveals the true power of these ancient practices. Once the initial crisis of disconnection passes, once we stop grasping for external guidance and begin to settle into stillness, the dormant capacities we've always possessed start to reawaken naturally. The process follows a predictable progression that our ancestors would have recognized immediately.

First comes earth sensitivity—the ability to feel the subtle energies that move through the environment. What begins as simple breath awareness expands into feeling the tremors and vibrations that most people never notice. The ground beneath our feet becomes alive with information, the air itself carries messages about weather changes and seasonal shifts hours before they become visible to the untrained eye.

Then develops human energy awareness. The capacity to distinguish people by the unique signature of their footsteps returns—some walking with the confident crunch of someone comfortable in the wilderness, others moving with the lighter, more tentative rhythm of those still finding their footing. Each person carries their own energetic frequency that becomes as recognizable as their voice, sometimes more so.

The auditory landscape expands dramatically. What once registered as generic "nature sounds" reveals itself as a complex symphony of specific communications. The rustling of different types of leaves, the distinct calls of various birds, the subtle hum of insects responding to changes in humidity and temperature—all become part of a vast information network we're suddenly able to access again.

Perhaps most remarkably, the ability to sense energy across distance begins to return. The kind of awareness that allows you to feel someone's presence before seeing them, to sense emotional states from across a field, to know when you're being observed even when no logical cues are available. This isn't mystical phenomena—it's the restoration of perceptual capacities that humans relied on for survival for millennia.

The breakthrough often comes through unexpected moments of authentic human connection. When the careful masks we wear in daily life begin to dissolve, we start to perceive people not through the filters of our expectations but through direct energetic contact. A stern authority figure reveals the gentle heart beneath their protective exterior. An intimidating presence shows unexpected kindness and humor. We begin to read the essence of people rather than just their surface presentations.

This wasn't mystical or otherworldly—it was the return of sensitivities that all humans once possessed. Our ancestors survived by reading environmental cues, tracking subtle changes, staying attuned to the intelligence that flows through the natural world. They knew that true guidance doesn't come from outside devices but from remembering how to listen to the wisdom that's always available when we become still enough to receive it.

The most remarkable thing was how quickly this capacity returned, as if I was remembering a language I'd spoken fluently as a child. We all have moments when we sense something before it happens, when we know to trust our gut feeling, when we wake up thinking of someone just before they call. These aren't coincidences —they're glimpses of the vast communication network we're always part of.

The difference between modern anxiety and ancient listening is surprisingly simple: one comes from being cut off from our inner guidance, the other from remembering that we're never actually alone or without direction. When we learn to read the subtle intelligence that flows through our bodies, our environment, and our intuition, we discover that we have access to exactly the guidance we need.

This doesn't require moving to a forest or becoming a monk. It starts with creating small moments of stillness in your day—perhaps a few minutes of breath awareness before checking your phone in the morning, or pausing to actually notice your surroundings instead of moving through life on autopilot. The ancient ones understood that the most sophisticated guidance system we possess isn't in our devices but in our capacity to be present with what's actually happening right now.

The conversation between you and the larger intelligence of life never stopped. We simply got so busy listening to external noise that we forgot how to hear it. But like any language we once knew well, it comes back to us quickly once we remember that we already know how to listen.

The ancient ones are still speaking. The question is: are you ready to listen?

Chapter 7
Reclaiming the Forgotten Language

Watch a three-year-old encounter a butterfly for the first time. Notice how naturally they accept its presence as meaningful, how they might whisper secrets to it or follow it with the unshakeable conviction that it has something important to show them. They don't question whether butterflies can carry messages or wonder if their interpretation is scientifically valid. They simply know that beauty and meaning are intertwined, that the world speaks in symbols, that everything is connected in ways that don't require adult explanation.

We're all born fluent in this language.

Before we learn to read words, we read signs. Before we understand logical cause and effect, we understand the poetry of meaningful coincidence. Before we're taught that random is random, we know that patterns carry intelligence, that repetition signals importance, that the universe has a way of arranging encounters between souls and symbols at precisely the moments when guidance is most needed.

Then we grow up. We learn that coincidence is just coincidence, that meaning is something we project onto meaningless events, that the language of symbol and synchronicity is primitive thinking we need to outgrow. We become sophisticated in our dismissal of the very experiences that once felt like direct communication from the source of all knowing.

But the unconscious mind—what Carl Jung called the realm of the collective unconscious—never stops speaking in symbols. Jung understood that consciousness operates on multiple levels simultaneously, that beneath our rational everyday awareness flows a vast reservoir of archetypal wisdom that communicates through images, patterns, and meaningful coincidences that bypass the skeptical mind and speak directly to the soul.

Jung recognized that numbers carry what he called "archetypal significance"—vibrational meanings that speak to something deep in human consciousness. When the same numbers appear repeatedly, you're receiving communication from what he called the Self—the organizing principle that guides individual development toward wholeness.

This truth revealed itself during one of the most devastating periods of my life, when loss forced me to pay attention to patterns I'd previously dismissed.

Both my beloved dog Raychel's first seizure and my aunt's death occurred on January 11th. Raychel then held on for exactly nineteen more days, passing on the 29th—

2 plus 9 equals 11. The same day my aunt's body arrived in the Philippines for her funeral. When I looked up my life path number in numerology, I discovered it was also 11—a number traditionally associated with spiritual awakening, intuition, and new beginnings.

These weren't coincidences I was desperately trying to find meaning in. They were patterns so impossible to ignore that even my rational mind had to acknowledge something larger was orchestrating events with mathematical precision. It felt like Raychel had agreed to a divine plan, her passing marking the end of one chapter of my life and the beginning of something I couldn't yet understand but was being called to trust.

The synchronicities didn't stop there. On the day I lost my job—another unexpected ending that felt like the universe dismantling everything I thought I knew about my future—a brown butterfly appeared on my ceiling. It stayed there for hours, this impossible messenger that had somehow found its way into my room, appearing at the exact moment I needed to remember that transformation often looks like loss before it reveals itself as liberation.

Later, when grief felt unbearable and I was questioning everything, I found myself scrolling through YouTube and discovering a video of a dog psychic whose words felt like they were spoken directly to my broken heart: "Animals offer us an opportunity to understand family in a way that we wish we could understand our own families. By being present for them in their final stage, we're getting to experience being of service, we get to experience unconditional love... Is it painful? Yes. Is it beautiful? Yeah. And it is also really perfect."

Those words arrived at precisely the moment I needed to hear them, carried by the invisible intelligence that Jung understood orchestrates such encounters. The psychic wasn't speaking generally about animals—she was speaking to me about Raychel, about the sacred gift hidden within devastating loss, about the curriculum of love that my dog's nineteen-day vigil had been designed to teach.

This is how the forgotten language operates—not through linear logic but through meaningful coincidence. Jung understood that consciousness arranges encounters between souls and exactly the guidance they need, delivered through whatever symbols are available.

At an ayahuasca ceremony, a woman approached me afterward, recognizing something in my energy. "What's your Life Path number? Let me guess—11?" She wasn't making a lucky guess but demonstrating the intuitive recognition that happens when we remember how to read energetic signatures. "We recognize our own," she said with a knowing smile. "I'm an 11 too."

Ancient wisdom traditions understood what Jung rediscovered through psychology: that individual consciousness is connected to universal consciousness through archetypal patterns that manifest as symbols, dreams, synchronicities, and meaningful encounters. The Aboriginal Australians speak of the Dreamtime—a parallel reality where all events are connected through invisible threads of meaning. Hindu and Buddhist traditions describe the akashic records—the cosmic library where every soul's journey is written in symbolic language that transcends ordinary time and space.

These weren't primitive superstitions but sophisticated recognition that consciousness extends far beyond the boundaries of individual minds, that meaning isn't something we create but something we learn to recognize in patterns that were always there.

The key to reclaiming this forgotten language is developing what Jung called "active imagination"—receptive attention that allows patterns to emerge naturally. It's simpler than it sounds.

For the next week, keep a small notebook and jot down what repeats: number sequences on clocks or receipts, animals crossing your path unusually, themes in dreams or conversations, songs that seem to answer unspoken questions. Don't analyze—just notice. Patterns reveal themselves through gentle attention, not forced interpretation.

Pay attention to timing. The perfect book falling off a shelf when you need its message. The overheard conversation answering your unspoken question. The song that speaks to your exact situation just as you're questioning which direction to take.

Trust your dreams as direct communication from the unconscious mind that accesses information beyond waking awareness. Your body carries subtle intelligence too—notice the contraction when considering wrong paths, the expansion when moving toward your purpose.

Most importantly, symbolic communication isn't

about universal meanings but about relationship with patterns in your unique life. The same symbol carries different messages for different people, even for the same person at different times. What matters isn't objective interpretation but felt recognition—that sense of "this is important" even when you can't explain why.

Jung understood that we're living through a time of collective awakening, when more and more people are remembering capacities that seemed lost to modernity. Perhaps this is why so many of us have been carrying that unnamed yearning, that soul ache for something we couldn't identify. We weren't broken or ungrateful—we were remembering a language we once knew fluently, feeling the absence of the symbolic conversation that once made our ancestors feel held by an intelligent universe.

When we reclaim this forgotten language, something profound happens: the ache begins to heal. The sense of isolation that comes from believing we live in a random, meaningless world starts to dissolve. We remember that we're not alone, that we're part of an ongoing conversation with the larger intelligence that moves through all things. The very yearning that felt like spiritual homesickness was actually our soul remembering its native tongue—the symbolic dialogue through which the universe has always been speaking to those willing to listen.

The rational mind, for all its gifts, was never meant to be consciousness's only tool. It was meant to collaborate with intuition, creativity, and the mysterious intelligence that Jung called the transcendent function—the capacity to receive guidance from sources that transcend individual knowing.

The language hasn't disappeared. We've simply forgotten how to listen. But like any language we once spoke fluently, it returns to us quickly once we remember that we never actually lost the ability to understand it.

Your dreams are still speaking. Numbers are still carrying vibrational messages. Animals are still appearing as messengers. Your body is still receiving intuitive information. The same intelligence that orchestrated Raychel's nineteen-day teaching, that brought the butterfly to my ceiling at the moment of greatest uncertainty, that arranged for the dog psychic's words to find me in my darkest hour—that intelligence is weaving meaning through your life every single day.

The conversation was never interrupted. We simply got distracted by louder voices. But in the quiet spaces between thoughts, in the pause before making important decisions, in the moments when synchronicity makes us stop and wonder—the ancient dialogue continues.

We are being spoken to. We are being guided. We are being loved through a language older than words, more reliable than logic, more intimate than any human conversation.

The question isn't whether you're fluent in symbolic communication. The question is: are you ready to trust what you've always known how to read?

Chapter 8
The Courage to Trust Again

Six months after sitting in silence for ten days, I found myself staring at an unexpected sum of money in my bank account. Severance pay, plus a bonus I never saw coming. The HR representative had been clear when she delivered the layoff news: "You won't receive any special bonus because this is a formal separation from the company, essentially a legal dismissal." Her words had stung with their corporate efficiency, matter-of-fact and final.

But there it was—an additional payment that shouldn't have existed according to her explanation, sitting in my account like a gentle correction to her certainty. The universe, it seemed, was placing resources in my hands just as I stood at the crossroads of an impossible choice: trust the writing path that had been calling me since 2022, or find another "sensible" job.

The brown butterfly had appeared months earlier when my old life fell apart, confirming that some endings are actually beginnings in disguise. Now here I was, holding the financial remnants of that same ending—money that had once represented security in a life I was meant to outgrow, now transformed into fuel for a journey I was meant to take. But confirmation and courage are different creatures entirely. One whispers recognition; the other demands action.

There's a particular kind of terror that accompanies spiritual knowing. It's not the fear of the unknown—it's the fear of what we already know to be true. When the soul speaks clearly, we can no longer claim ignorance. We can no longer hide behind the comfortable confusion of not knowing what we're meant to do. The path becomes visible, and with visibility comes responsibility.

Bali. The name had been circling my consciousness since that online course two years prior, along with Egypt and London—destinations that felt less like vacation spots and more like coordinates for an inner mapping I didn't yet understand. March arrived with its familiar birthday energy, that annual invitation to begin again, and suddenly the calling became urgent. COVID restrictions had finally lifted. The timing felt orchestrated.

This wasn't the old kind of travel, the kind that chases external experiences to fill internal voids. This was different. This was pilgrimage.

The money felt like a message: *Use this. Trust this journey.*

And trust—I was learning—requires a different kind of courage than we're taught to cultivate. We're trained to be brave in measurable ways—to take calculated risks, to have backup plans, to move forward only when we can see the entire staircase illuminated. Spiritual courage asks something else entirely. It asks us to take the first step when we can only see that single step, trusting that the light will move with us.

Yet every wisdom tradition throughout history has pointed toward the same truth: there's an intelligence beyond the intellect, a knowing that doesn't come from accumulating information but from accessing something already present within us. Learning to trust this inner guidance may be the most radical act of faith we can undertake in a world that demands proof before belief.

I had been building this capacity slowly through previous travel experiences, each one teaching me that following seemingly illogical nudges often leads to exactly what we need, even when we don't know what that is.

Now, faced with this unexpected windfall and the persistent call of Bali, I found myself at a familiar crossroads. My practical mind catalogued all the sensible alternatives: update the resume, network with former colleagues, leverage my corporate experience into another stable position. The money in my account could serve as a safety net while job hunting, not fuel for what others might see as an extended vacation disguised as spiritual seeking.

But something had shifted during those ten days of silence. The voice that once whispered hesitantly now spoke with quiet certainty. I had learned to recognize the difference between the anxious chatter of the thinking mind and the calm knowing that rises from deeper wells. This wasn't escapism or avoidance. This was following a thread that I was finally brave enough to hold.

So when April arrived with its familiar invitation to begin again, I found myself making a choice that surprised even me.

I booked a ticket to Bali.

Not as a vacation or escape, but as an act of faith. April came, and I found myself on a plane carrying nothing but a backpack and the growing understanding that when we align with our deepest knowing, the world responds in ways we could never orchestrate through planning alone.

The first few days in Bali felt like stepping into a different frequency entirely. The island's energy was palpable—something about the way morning light filtered through palm leaves, the sound of temple bells carried on tropical breeze, the gentle warmth of people who seemed to move through life with an unhurried knowing. I found myself slowing down, paying attention to subtleties I'd been too busy to notice in my previous travels. I wanted to experience Bali myself, not just pass through it like another destination on a checklist. This meant wandering without agenda, sitting in cafes until conversations naturally arose, following impulses to explore temples that weren't in any guidebook. There was something about the island that invited a different way of being—less doing, more receiving. Less planning, more trusting.

It was during one of these early mornings, following an impulse to witness sunrise from sacred ground, that I found myself standing before Mount Agung as it rose through morning mist like a sleeping giant slowly awakening. One of Bali's four sacred mountains, revered for centuries as a pillar connecting earth and sky. Getting there had been its own lesson in trust—a journey made possible by a travel guide I'd found through the most unlikely synchronicity: a random stranger on Reddit who shared a WhatsApp number for someone reliable and affordable. Even the path to the sacred mountain arrived through unexpected channels.

The clouds had been thick all morning, obscuring the mountain's peak. Other tourists clustered at the viewpoint, cameras ready, all of us waiting for that perfect moment. *If I'm meant to be here,* I thought, *if this path I'm walking is real, show me.* It wasn't a demand or an ultimatum—it was the quiet prayer of someone learning to dialogue with mystery.

I waited with the others, watching the sky. Then, gradually over the course of ten minutes, the clouds began to dissipate. Not suddenly, but steadily, as if responding to some gentle cosmic choreography. By the time it was my turn to step forward for photos, the mountain stood revealed in full majesty, clear and proud against blue sky, as if the universe had been orchestrating this moment of perfect timing all along.

Standing there with my camera, I felt something shift in my understanding of how guidance works. Not because they prove anything to anyone else, but because they remind us that we're in conversation with something larger than our isolated understanding. They whisper that perhaps the universe is more responsive, more aware, more intimately connected to our journey than we dared to imagine.

What followed was a cascade of confirmations that felt like a master class in synchronicity. Melton appeared just as I was questioning my next destination—a half-Filipino man from London who seemed to materialize exactly when I needed to hear his perspective. "Bali is like a melting pot," he explained with the wisdom of someone who'd witnessed countless transformations. "Different kinds of people come here for different reasons—some for relationships, some for the next step in life, some running from something, others running toward something they can't yet name. But the island has a way of giving everyone exactly what they need, even when it's not what they expected."

He studied my face with knowing eyes. "What you experience here in Bali," he told me during one of those conversations that feel orchestrated by something beyond coincidence, "is something you will bring with you for the rest of your life. Not as a memory, but as a new way of being. The island doesn't just show you beautiful places—it shows you parts of yourself you forgot existed."

His words proved prophetic in ways I couldn't have imagined. Almost as if responding to his prediction, the island began presenting me with exactly the teachers and experiences I needed. The guides who found me seemed chosen by some invisible hand. One treated me like a younger brother, taking me to places that weren't on any tourist map, sharing stories and insights that felt like gifts

The Real Rayster

I hadn't earned. Another appeared with a vintage convertible—one of those classic cars with the removable windshield and manual everything—and spent hours showing me hidden temples and secret beaches.

At the monkey forest, he warned me with a grin, "Keep your belongings close. These guys are professional thieves." Sure enough, we watched as a particularly mischievous monkey spotted another visitor's water bottle and made his move with the calculated precision of a seasoned pickpocket. The guide laughed as we witnessed the gentle tug-of-war between tourist and creature, the monkey seeming to enjoy the game far more than his victim. "Even the monkeys here teach lessons about letting go," my guide chuckled as we watched the scene unfold. "Sometimes you have to surrender what you think you need to discover what you actually need."

Every practical need was met before I even recognized I had it. Every question was answered by the next person I encountered. Every moment of uncertainty was followed by such clear guidance that I began to understand what the ancients meant when they spoke of being led by forces greater than the individual will.

But this wasn't just a series of lucky coincidences or well-timed meetings. Something deeper was being revealed about the nature of trust itself. Week after week in Bali, I found myself witnessing what I can only call magic—not the theatrical kind that demands disbelief suspended, but the quiet kind that invites recognition of intelligence woven into the fabric of existence itself.

I was beginning to believe in magic again, the way

children believe before the world teaches them to doubt their own knowing. Not the magic of wishful thinking or spiritual bypassing, but the magic of alignment—when we stop forcing outcomes and start following the current of what wants to emerge through us.

Bali became a perfect place for me to assess what I wanted to do next, not through analysis or strategic planning, but through feeling into what felt alive and what felt dead. The island's slower rhythm allowed space for deeper currents to surface, for the voice beneath the voice to finally be heard above the chatter of should and supposed to.

In this environment, surrounded by a culture that honored the sacred in daily life, I could feel what direction wanted to emerge next without the noise of other people's expectations drowning out my own knowing. The island didn't just give me permission to trust my path—it gave me evidence that the path was trustworthy.

Here's what I learned about spiritual courage in those Balinese moments: it's not a one-time decision. It's a daily, hourly, sometimes moment-by-moment choice to keep trusting what we know to be true, even when fear whispers louder than faith.

This understanding crystallized for me in a moment of perfect stillness on that sacred mountain.

Standing there, watching clouds dance with peaks older than human memory, I felt something shift inside me. Not a dramatic conversion, but a quiet settling into trust. The voice that had been whispering about writing, about sharing, about using words to build bridges between worlds—that voice wasn't leading me astray. It was leading me home.

The confirmation didn't come before the courage. The confirmation came because of the courage. Because I chose to trust the money that arrived against all predictions, the inner knowing that persisted despite practical objections, the call that wouldn't be silenced no matter how impractical it seemed.

When we finally stop asking for proof before we leap, we discover that the net appears not to catch us from falling, but to support us in flying. We learn that spiritual courage isn't about eliminating fear—it's about choosing trust as our primary relationship with uncertainty.

The real magic of Bali wasn't in the synchronicities, though they were beautiful. The real magic was in discovering that when we align with our deepest knowing and take action from that place, the world reveals itself as far more alive, aware, and supportive than we ever dared to believe.

This is where the alchemy happens: when trust becomes the bridge between receiving guidance and expressing it in the world. When we stop protecting our creative impulses and start following them. When we realize that trusting our inner knowing isn't the end of the journey—it's the beginning of everything we came here to create and share.

The path home to ourselves is always a path of trust. And trust, it turns out, is not something we feel—it's something we practice. Each time we choose to listen rather than analyze, to follow rather than control, to say yes to the mystery rather than demand it reveal all its secrets first.

When we learn to trust deeply enough, something extraordinary happens: we don't just receive guidance—we become it. We don't just follow the creative impulse—we embody it. We discover that the courage to trust our inner knowing naturally flows into the courage to share our unique gifts with a world that desperately needs what only we can offer. This is how trust transforms from personal practice into sacred expression, how the conversation with mystery becomes the wellspring from which all authentic creativity flows.

Chapter 9
Creating from a Listening Heart

When we learn to trust that inner voice, something remarkable happens—we become conduits for creation itself. Not the frantic kind that comes from trying to prove ourselves, but the kind that flows when we remember we're not separate from the creative force moving through all things.

This is why creative expression heals the soul ache so many of us carry. When we create from a listening heart, we remember our connection to the source of all creativity. The unnamed yearning that felt like emptiness reveals itself as the very space through which inspiration flows. We discover that what we thought was broken was actually an opening—a sacred receptivity that allows life to create through us in ways we never imagined possible.

Every time we follow a creative impulse—whether it's writing a poem, arranging flowers, solving a problem with fresh insight, or simply speaking our truth in conversation—we participate in the healing of the world's forgotten wholeness. We remember that we belong, that our unique way of seeing and expressing matters, that we're part of the vast creative intelligence that moves through all things.

There's an ancient understanding that creation itself is *Lila*—divine play. When we create from a listening heart, we participate in this cosmic dance, becoming instruments through which life expresses its endless creativity for the sheer joy of it.

Ancient traditions knew this secret. Indigenous storytellers understood they weren't the source of their stories but vessels through which ancestral wisdom found voice. Islamic calligraphers cultivated inner stillness so divine beauty could flow through human hands onto paper. Each letter became prayer, each word a bridge between worlds.

This same recognition lives in small moments—the steam rising from freshly whisked matcha, green powder settling into stillness as morning quiet holds space for what wants to emerge. I've learned to recognize how ideas arrive—not as thoughts I generate but as gifts that present themselves when my mind grows quiet enough to receive them. For years, I carried fragments in scattered notes, phrases that appeared while walking, insights between sleep and waking. These were recognitions that came through openness rather than effort.

But you don't need to be a traditional artist to participate in this conversation between spirit and matter.

Every moment offers opportunities for creation from a listening heart.

The way you arrange your living space, responding to what feels harmonious rather than following magazine layouts. The way you prepare a meal, letting seasonal ingredients guide the flavors rather than rigidly following recipes. The way you solve problems at work by pausing to sense what the situation actually needs rather than applying standard formulas.

Even conversation becomes creative practice when we speak from genuine listening rather than rehearsed opinions. The words that emerge often surprise us—carrying wisdom we didn't know we possessed.

Most of us have been trained to think creativity belongs only to "artists," as if the capacity to translate inspiration into form were rare rather than our birthright. But consider the creativity in daily existence: intuitively knowing how to comfort a friend, solutions arising when you stop forcing, the perfect timing of encounters that offer exactly the guidance you need.

This is creation happening through you—intelligence expressing itself through your unique way of being. When we recognize this, work transforms from forcing predetermined outcomes to collaborating with what wants to emerge, technique serving something larger than personal achievement.

Returning from travels through Japan and Taiwan, witnessing gardens tended with reverence and villages painted from pure joy, I felt something stirring—not the old need to achieve but a yearning to serve, to become skilled enough that insights gained through experience could find clear expression.

This is what becomes possible when we approach our careers, our relationships, our daily choices as creative acts—opportunities to listen deeply and respond from that place of inner knowing rather than external expectations. Whether we're writing emails or writing books, raising children or planting gardens, the same principle applies: creation flows most freely when we become curious about what wants to emerge rather than attached to what we think should happen.

The question isn't whether you're creative—you are, simply by virtue of being alive, conscious, responsive to beauty and meaning. The question is whether you're willing to trust the conversation between your deepest listening and the world's need for exactly what wants to emerge through your unique way of seeing, feeling, and expressing.

This kind of creative expression becomes especially important for those who feel the world's pain deeply, who carry sensitivity as both gift and burden. When we learn to channel our deep feeling into creative acts—whether that's writing, gardening, problem-solving, or simply offering presence to others—we transform our sensitivity from something that overwhelms us into something that heals both ourselves and the world. This is how the tender-hearted become agents of gentle revolution, how those who feel too much discover their feelings are exactly the medicine the world needs.

In a world hungry for authentic expression, for solutions that arise from wisdom rather than cleverness, for beauty that nourishes rather than merely decorates, your willingness to create from a listening heart isn't just personal fulfillment—it's medicine the world is waiting to receive.

For the next week, try this gentle experiment: before creating anything—writing an email, preparing dinner, starting a project, even choosing what to wear—pause for a moment and ask silently, "What wants to be expressed through me right now?" Notice the difference between forcing and flowing, between creation as effort and creation as response to what's calling to emerge.

Pay attention to the moments when time seems to disappear, when you lose yourself in the joy of making something beautiful or useful or meaningful. These aren't escapes from real life—they're glimpses of what becomes possible when we remember that we are not separate from the creative force that moves through all things.

The ancient ones knew this secret: we are all participants in the grand *Lila* of existence, each contributing our verse to the cosmic poem that consciousness writes through countless awakening hearts. The masterpiece isn't what we make—it's what we become when we remember how to listen deeply enough to let life create through us.

Chapter 10
Sacred Rebels, Soft Warriors

The morning news streams its familiar litany of crisis and conflict while you sip your coffee, feeling the weight of a world that seems to be forgetting its own heart. Something in you wants to turn away, to protect your sensitive spirit from the sharpness of humanity's collective pain. But another part of you—the part that has learned to listen—recognizes this moment of overwhelm as a sacred invitation.

I know this temptation intimately. I've watched my father's pain turn into rage, felt betrayal slice through trust like a blade, experienced heartbreak that whispered seductive promises about the safety of walls. There were moments when closing my heart felt like the only sane response to a world that seemed determined to wound anyone brave enough to remain open.

But something always called me back—a quiet voice that said the world needs people willing to stay soft. Not because it's easy, but because someone has to keep the light on. Someone has to prove that love is stronger than fear, that gentleness isn't weakness, that an open heart in a hardening world is exactly what's needed.

Revolution doesn't always announce itself with raised fists. Sometimes it whispers through the tears of a cashier who feels truly seen because you took an extra moment to really look at her. Sometimes it spreads like ripples when you choose presence over productivity, refusing to hurry through your own life.

The world doesn't need you to fix everything. It needs you to remember that your sensitivity is actually your sacred assignment.

You are not broken for feeling too much in a world that celebrates numbing. You are not naive for choosing love when everything around you argues for cynicism. You are not powerless simply because your weapons are softness and your battlefield is consciousness itself.

In a small café in a city that could be anywhere, a woman sits across from her teenage daughter, both of them present for perhaps the first time in months. No phones, no distractions, just two human beings remembering how to see each other. Neither knows that their moment of authentic connection is witnessed by a stranger at the next table, who carries this glimpse of genuine love home to her own family, where it sparks a different kind of conversation over dinner that night.

The sacred rebels understand that their real work is internal—choosing to stay open when everything encourages closing, staying connected to compassion when cynicism would be easier, keeping faith in humanity's goodness when the evidence seems scarce.

This is how soft warriors heal their own soul ache—not by fixing themselves in isolation, but by discovering that their deepest healing happens through service to others. When we use our sensitivity to hold space for someone else's pain, when we offer our presence to a world that desperately needs witnessing, when we choose to be a healing force rather than another source of disconnection, something profound occurs: the very ache that once felt like a wound transforms into a sacred opening through which love flows into the world.

The yearning that drove us to seek connection, understanding, and meaning finds its fulfillment not in finally feeling "fixed" but in becoming conduits for the healing the world needs. We discover that we were never broken—we were simply being prepared to serve as bridges between what is and what wants to become.

They know that healing the world begins with refusing to perpetuate the patterns of separation they want to see changed. Every person who learns to stay open makes it easier for the next person to choose love over fear.

Watch a tree in a windstorm. It doesn't resist by becoming harder; it survives by becoming more flexible, by rooting deeper, by trusting its own strength to bend without breaking. The oak that refuses to yield snaps in the storm, but the willow that knows how to dance with difficulty emerges even more graceful than before.

This is the way of the soft warrior—not passive, but

responsive. Not weak, but wise enough to know that the deepest transformation happens through connection, not conquest. Through embodying the change so completely that others remember what's possible when human beings dare to live from their wholeness.

The soft warriors don't wait for the world to become safe enough for their tenderness. They bring their tenderness to the world as it is, trusting that love is stronger than fear not because it overpowers opposition but because it dissolves the very foundation that makes opposition necessary.

In the grocery store, an elderly man struggles with his wallet while impatient customers shift behind him. The soft warrior doesn't sigh or check her phone. Instead, she steps forward with a warm smile, offers to help, and engages him in gentle conversation. Later, the cashier tells her coworker about the customer who made her whole day brighter just by being kind. The kindness ripples.

This is how consciousness changes—not through grand gestures but through millions of small choices to respond from love rather than react from fear, to see others as spiritual beings having human experiences rather than obstacles to navigate around.

What if the most radical thing you could do is simply refuse to abandon yourself—refuse to betray your deep knowing, refuse to pretend that productivity matters more than presence, refuse to accept that sensitivity is weakness in a world that has forgotten how to feel?

What if your willingness to stay open, to choose love over fear in the countless small moments of your ordinary days, is exactly the medicine our collective human heart needs right now?

The ancient mysteries taught that every awakened heart serves as a lighthouse, its very presence helping others remember their way home to themselves. You don't need to see the immediate results of your choice to live consciously. Your only job is to keep your inner light burning bright, trusting that your commitment to presence serves the whole in ways your mind may never fully understand.

Take a moment right now. Feel the quiet courage that moves through you when you dare to trust your deepest knowing. Notice the way love wants to express itself through your unique gifts, your particular sensitivity, your specific way of seeing and being.

This is your sacred rebellion: the choice to remain tender in a hardening world, to keep listening when the noise grows loud, to trust that your presence matters even when you can't see all the ways it's making a difference.

The world is waiting for your particular medicine, your unique contribution to the healing that wants to happen through awakening hearts. You are not too sensitive for this world. You are sensitive enough to help it remember what it means to be truly alive.

Chapter 11
When the World Starts to Listen Again

The signs are already here, scattered like seeds of hope across a world that's beginning to remember.

In Vienna, a small café hangs a simple sign: "No phones. No devices. Books and conversation only." The first day, three people come. By the third week, there's a waiting list. Strangers look up from novels to ask about favorite authors. Elderly women share stories with young fathers. The quiet revolution of presence spreads, one conversation at a time, as people rediscover the radical act of being fully with each other.

In Appleton, Wisconsin, something even more profound is taking root. Downtown, where busy people once hurried past each other without eye contact, stands a permanent space called the Community Living Room. The door reads "No appointments, no forms required"—just trained listeners and comfortable chairs where anyone can walk in carrying the weight of whatever they're facing. Visitors describe feeling "welcomed like family." In a world that medicates loneliness and monetizes connection, this simple space offers something revolutionary: the healing power of being truly heard.

Eight hundred miles away, the Northeast Stockton Library prepares to open with an intentional design that would mystify librarians from just a generation ago. Alongside the books stand comfortable conversation circles, communal tables designed for lingering, and quiet alcoves where strangers can become neighbors. It's part of a movement sweeping across the country—88% of public libraries now offer spaces specifically designed for authentic human connection. They've become sanctuaries for something our efficiency-obsessed culture nearly lost: the art of unhurried presence with one another.

Even our workplaces are remembering how to listen. When Google's researchers studied what makes teams most effective, they discovered something that surprised them: the single most important factor wasn't talent or resources or experience. It was psychological safety—the sense that people could speak their truth without fear. Now companies from Microsoft to small startups are learning what indigenous cultures always knew: that real collaboration requires spaces where every voice can be heard without judgment.

These aren't isolated experiments. They're symptoms of a deeper awakening, signs that the soul ache you've been carrying—that unnamed longing for authentic connection—isn't personal pathology but collective prophecy. The emptiness that drove you to these pages is the same emptiness driving communities everywhere to create new ways of being together.

The movement is slow, yes. Gradual as dawn breaking over a sleeping world. But it's happening.

What we're witnessing is the return of the soft warriors—people who understand that true strength lies not in forcing change but in creating spaces where change can emerge naturally. They're the café owners who risk profit margins to prioritize presence. The librarians who design for lingering instead of efficiency. The managers who choose vulnerability over authority. The neighbors who tend community gardens like temples.

Look for them in your own corner of the world. They might be the teacher who creates circle time for sharing instead of rushing through curriculum. The store owner who greets regulars by name and asks about their families. The friend who puts away her phone when you're talking and gives you the gift of her complete attention.

These quiet revolutionaries understand that healing our collective disconnection happens one relationship at a time, one moment of authentic presence at a time, one choice to listen deeply at a time.

And you? You who have felt the ache, who have longed for something more real than the scripts we've been handed, who have trusted enough to journey through these pages? You are already part of this awakening. Your willingness to feel deeply in a numbing world, to seek connection in a disconnecting culture, to trust that listening matters—this isn't personal healing but collective medicine.

When the World Forgot to Listen

Trust that your sensitivity serves a purpose larger than your individual comfort. Every time you pause before reacting, you create space for wisdom to emerge. Every time you ask "What is really needed here?" instead of "What's the fastest solution?" you participate in the great return to sacred timing. Every time you choose depth over speed, presence over productivity, connection over convenience, you vote for the world you want to live in.

Look for the other soft warriors already at work around you. They might be the librarian arranging chairs in circles instead of rows. The coworker who actually listens during coffee breaks. The neighbor who tends their garden like a meditation. These are your people—the ones who understand that the most revolutionary act in a disconnected world is learning to be genuinely present with whatever arises.

Begin where you are, with what you have. Create one small space—physical or relational—where people can speak their truth and know they'll be heard. It might be your living room, your lunch table, your corner of the office. It might serve two people or twenty. The size doesn't matter. What matters is the quality of listening you bring to it.

I dream of the moment when this remembering reaches what Malcolm Gladwell called "the tipping point"—when enough individuals have returned to listening that it begins to shift how our whole culture operates. When compassion becomes more valued than competition. When wisdom is sought as eagerly as data.

When "success" is measured not just by what we've accumulated, but by how much beauty we've created, how much suffering we've eased, how much love we've allowed to flow through us into the world.

Perhaps that moment won't arrive in my lifetime. Perhaps it will unfold slowly, like consciousness itself—mysteriously, unevenly, with setbacks and breakthroughs that can't be plotted on any linear timeline.

But I have hope because I've seen what happens when even one person chooses to listen deeply. How it changes the quality of their presence. How others feel safer to reveal their own truth in response. How small circles of authentic connection create ripples that expand in ways we can rarely track but somehow always feel.

The world is starting to listen again because people like you are choosing to remember. In quiet moments of morning stillness. In the courage to follow inner guidance that makes no logical sense. In the willingness to trust that your sensitivity serves a purpose larger than your individual healing.

The ancient ones knew something we're only beginning to remember: that listening is not passive but creative, not empty but full of potential, not weakness but the deepest form of strength. When we listen—to ourselves, to each other, to the living world around us—we participate in the ongoing creation of reality itself.

The silence you've been avoiding really is the answer you seek. Not because it holds specific instructions, but because it holds space for the wisdom that already lives within you to finally speak. Not because it promises easy answers, but because it offers the kind of deep knowing that can navigate any complexity with grace.

The world is starting to listen again because you are starting to listen again. And in that choice—made fresh each morning, each moment, each breath—lies all the hope we need for the healing that wants to happen through us, as us, in service to the love that connects us all.

This is how we remember our way home. This is how we save each other. This is how we love the world back to life.

One listening heart at a time.

Review Request

In a world that has forgotten how to listen, your voice matters.

If this book has helped you remember the sound beneath all sounds, if it has stirred that unnamed yearning in your chest, or if it has reminded you that your sensitivity is actually your strength, please consider sharing your experience through a review.

Your words might be exactly what another seeking soul needs to hear. Whether this journey brought you recognition, healing, hope, or simply a moment of feeling truly seen, your honest reflection creates a bridge for others walking the path back to themselves.

Every review becomes part of the quiet revolution—helping fellow travelers find their way to the listening heart that changes everything. In a culture drowning in noise, your authentic voice adds to the chorus of remembering.

Review Request

Your story matters. Your listening heart matters. Your willingness to share this experience matters.

Please leave a review on:

- Amazon US
- Amazon UK
- Amazon CA
- Amazon AUS
- and other Amazon sites where you purchased this book!

or Scan the QR below

Together, we're helping the world remember how to listen again.

With gratitude for your open heart,
TheReal Rayster

References & Sources

Note: While this book is primarily a work of spiritual memoir and wisdom, certain statistics and research findings mentioned have been drawn from the following sources to provide context for our modern disconnection and emerging reconnection.

Digital Overwhelm & Modern Life:

- Smartphone usage statistics: Asurion consumer research studies (2019-2023)
- Information processing research: University of California San Diego studies on daily information consumption
- Attention economy research: Various studies on digital distraction and focus fragmentation

Psychological & Social Research:

- Gladwell, Malcolm. *The Tipping Point: How Little Things Can Make a Big Difference*. Little, Brown and Company, 2000.
- Google's Project Aristotle: Research on team effectiveness and psychological safety (2016)
- Library design and community connection: American Library Association reports on 21st-century library evolution

Spiritual & Psychological Traditions:

- Jung, Carl Gustav. Various works on the collective unconscious, active imagination, and archetypal psychology

References & Sources

- Vipassana meditation: Traditional Buddhist mindfulness practices as taught in the Goenka tradition
- Indigenous wisdom traditions: Various sources on traditional ways of reading environmental and spiritual signs

Personal Experiences:

- Retreat experiences and spiritual practices are drawn from the author's direct participation
- Synchronicities and meaningful coincidences are documented personal experiences
- Travel experiences in Bali and other locations are based on the author's journals and memories

This book prioritizes lived experience and intuitive wisdom over academic research. Where specific statistics are mentioned, they are intended to illustrate broader cultural patterns rather than serve as precise scientific claims.

Printed in Dunstable, United Kingdom